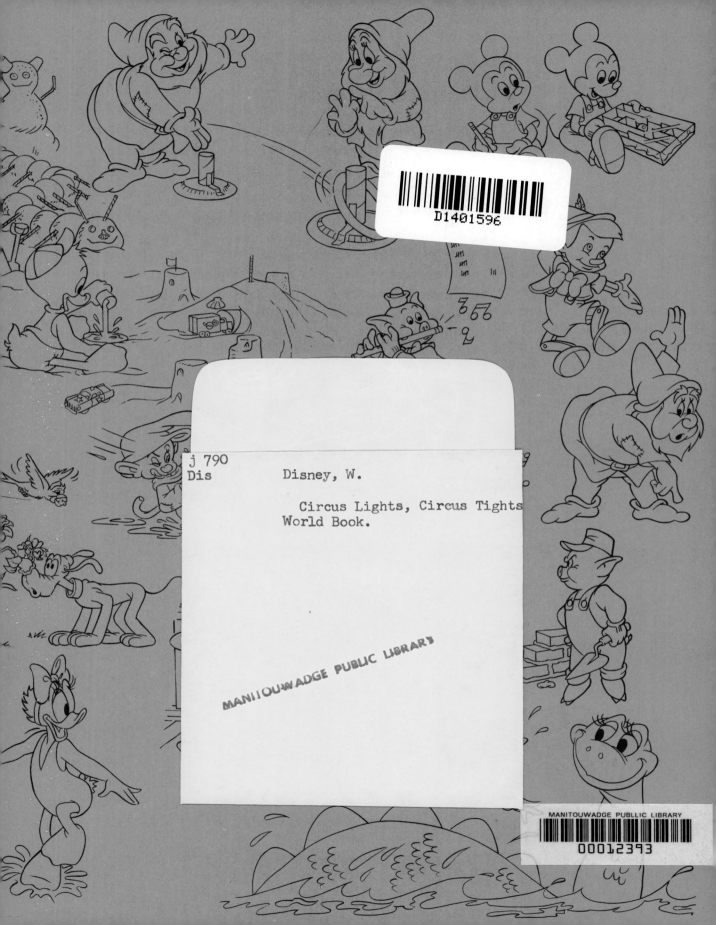

Note to Parents

Circus Lights, Circus Tights will take your child behind the scenes with Dumbo, the flying elephant, and his friend Timothy Mouse. The adventures of the two friends include handy tips for clown makeup, directions for magic tricks, and many other circus activities to try out and enjoy.

Some of the activities in this book are designed for indoor use and some for active outdoor play. Most can be done without close supervision. The Jiminy Cricket symbol appears with any project or activity that requires adult help.

The materials used in the activities in this book can be bought or found around the house. Old clothes, homemade grease paint, a few simple props, and a little imagination are all your child will need for hours of fun.

Activities with grease paint and popcorn can be messy. Before your child begins, provide him or her with a smock (an old shirt will do), and cover the work area with newspaper.

Of course, a circus is even more exciting when it's shared with friends. Expect some lively performances from a troupe of clowns, jugglers, and "tightrope walkers"— and enjoy the fun.

Circus Lights,
Circus Tights

Three-Ring Stunts and Capers

Published by
World Book Encyclopedia, Inc.
a Scott Fetzer company
Chicago

The Lost Circus

Usually Dumbo and Timothy loved riding the circus
train from town to town. They liked traveling with all of
their circus friends, and they enjoyed watching the
scenery as the train chugged along.

But one evening, after they had finished their show,
they had a long ride to get to the town where the next
show would be. And it was a rough ride! The train
started and stopped and rattled and banged and jiggled
and swayed all night long, and Dumbo and Timothy
couldn't sleep a wink. By the next morning, the two
friends were very, very tired.

"Dumbo," said Timothy, "why don't we fly to the
town where the circus will be? You fly a lot more
smoothly than the train runs—and if we get there
before the train does, we can take a little nap. How
about it?"

Dumbo looked a little doubtful. He wasn't really sure he could find the right town. "Don't worry, Dumbo," Timothy said. "I'll be your pilot and tell you which way to go. I have a good sense of direction."

So the next time the circus train jerked to a stop, Dumbo and Timothy climbed out. Timothy perched in Dumbo's hat, and they took off—up, up, up, circling higher and higher in the sky.

Timothy knew they could find the right town if they just followed the railroad tracks. So that's exactly what he and Dumbo did. But before long, they ran into heavy, dark clouds. Rain spattered in their faces, and the wind pushed them this way and that. It even spun them around! By the time Dumbo and Timothy got through the storm, the railroad tracks and the circus were nowhere in sight.

Dumbo felt so sad and worried that he couldn't keep on flying. He landed in the middle of a field and sat there, with his ears drooping.

"I'm sorry, Dumbo," Timothy said. "I didn't know this would happen. I guess we should have stayed with the circus train. But we can't be *very* lost. When you've had a rest, let's just fly back and forth until we find our circus again."

So they did. It wasn't long until they spotted a big building with a billboard next to it. On the billboard was a picture of a huge elephant with a curled trunk. "I'll bet that's it, Dumbo," Timothy said excitedly. "Land there!"

Dumbo landed—but there were no tents or clowns or animals around. All that he and Timothy found was a lot of moving vans, all with the same elephant picture. On each elephant picture was a sign that said, "From a trunkful to a houseful—we move your things fast!"

FAST

FROM A
TRUNKFUL
TO A HOUSEFUL
WE-MOVE
YOUR THINGS
FAST!

"This isn't the circus," Timothy said. "But don't worry, Dumbo. I'm sure we'll find it soon." So they took off again, up, up, up into the sky.

They had been flying only a few minutes when Timothy spotted a big, striped tent near a clump of trees. Lots of cars were parked nearby.

"Look, Dumbo," Timothy said, jumping up and down in Dumbo's hat. "I think we've found it!"

Dumbo was so excited that he swooped down and sailed right through the doorway of the big tent. He and Timothy landed . . . *plunk!* . . . right in the middle of the most enormous old bed they had ever seen.

"What are you doing!" a woman shouted as Dumbo and Timothy bounced to a standstill. "Get off that bed! It's an antique! You'll ruin it!"

Dumbo and Timothy looked around. The tent was full of people and furniture—old, beautiful, expensive furniture that the people had come to buy. Slowly and carefully, they got off the bed and tiptoed out of the tent. They didn't want to break anything!

Dumbo and Timothy took off again. For a long time
they flew back and forth without seeing anything.
Finally, Timothy spotted a big open space surrounded
by grandstands full of people. "I'm not sure, Dumbo,"
said Timothy, "but I think that's our circus ring. I
wonder what happened to the tent! Let's go and find out."

Dumbo swooped down and landed in the middle of
the ring. Everybody clapped and laughed—but then
someone yelled, "Look out, young fella!" Out of a gate
at the side of the ring thundered a big horse. It reared
and bucked and shook and snorted, while its rider hung
on for dear life!

"Oops—I think we've found a rodeo, Dumbo,"
Timothy said. "And that cowboy is having a rougher
ride than we had on the circus train."

"Hey, young fella with the ears," someone else yelled.
"You're in the wrong place! You'd better fly on over to
the circus. You've missed it by about a mile!"

"You hear that, Dumbo?" Timothy said. "The circus is
only a mile from here! I'm sure we can find it now."

Dumbo and Timothy took off again. Dumbo circled
slowly while Timothy looked all around. "There it is! I
see it!" cried Timothy.

Dumbo glided down, his ears spread wide. There was
the big, familiar tent—and there were all of his and
Timothy's good, good friends, waving and running to
meet them.

Of course, Timothy couldn't wait to tell about all of
their adventures, but Dumbo just sat in the sawdust of
the big circus ring and sighed happily. He had done all
of the flying and a lot of worrying, too—and he was
glad to be home.

Home Sweet TENT

9

The Board Walk

Dumbo really liked to watch the tightrope walkers. He watched them practice their act every day. One day after the tightrope walkers had finished practicing, Dumbo decided to try to walk the tightrope himself.

Of course, it wasn't hard for Dumbo to get up to the platform. He just flapped his ears and flew! But what a surprise Dumbo got when he tried tightrope-walking! The rope wasn't heavy enough to hold an elephant—even a little one. It stretched all the way to the floor—and there was Dumbo, back on the ground.

Dumbo found a way to practice tightrope walking without the tightrope. He got a long board and two bricks. Dumbo put each end of the board on a brick and walked back and forth on his board-and-brick "tightrope."

Dumbo added some tricks to his tightrope act. He learned to walk backward . . . to pick up a handkerchief . . . and to walk with an apple (or Timothy) balanced on his head. Of course, having a trunk made some of those tricks easy for Dumbo. Can you do them?

Make a Face

Just before showtime, Dumbo and Timothy went for a quick ride over the circus grounds.

"Oh, look," said Timothy. "There are the clowns, getting ready for the big show. Fly down there, Dumbo. Let's see what they're doing."

Dumbo straightened out his ears and they sailed down. All of the clowns were doing the same thing—they were using grease paint to make their clown faces. But each clown was making a different kind of face.

"Wow! I'd like to do that. Wouldn't you, Dumbo?" Timothy said. "With a little grease paint and some funny clothes, I'll bet we could be stars."

You can make grease paint and be a clown! Just follow the directions on the next page.

What you'll need

Small mixing bowl
Three small margarine
  tubs with lids
Fork

Mixing spoon
1 cup cornstarch
¾ cup vegetable shortening
Red and blue food coloring

1. Measure the cornstarch and put it in the mixing bowl.

2. Add the vegetable shortening to the cornstarch and mash it with the fork. Then stir the mixture with the mixing spoon until it is smooth and creamy.

3. Put half of the mixture into one margarine tub. Divide the other half equally between the other two tubs. Put the lid on the tub with the most mixture in it. (This is the white grease paint.)

4. Add red food coloring to one of the remaining tubs and blue to the other. Mix in a few drops at a time until you get the shade you want of each color.

Dumbo saw a clown face he really liked—and he wanted one just like it. He tapped Timothy gently with the tip of his trunk, to make him notice it.

"That *is* a nice face," said Timothy. "But you can't have a face exactly like that clown has. You see, every clown has a special face, and no other clown can use it. We'll have to make up special clown faces of our own."

So Dumbo and Timothy walked up and down Clown Alley, looking at the different kinds of faces—white-faced clowns and hobo clowns, smiling clowns and sad clowns. They saw all kinds of clown eyes and clown noses and clown hair. And pretty soon they knew exactly how they wanted to look.

Dumbo covered his whole face, except around his
eyes and his mouth, with white grease paint. He used
red grease paint to make a big, smiling mouth. Then he
used the blue grease paint to make big circles around
his eyes. (He was careful not to get the grease paint too
close to his eyes.) Timothy helped Dumbo paint the end
of his trunk red to make it look like a big, red nose.

Timothy wanted to be a sad-faced clown. He painted
on a big, sad mouth that curved down on each end. He
painted two red spots on his cheeks, and he used the
blue grease paint to make eyebrows. Timothy painted
the rest of his face with white grease paint and painted
a blue teardrop under each eye.

Suitable for a Clown

"We're beginning to look like clowns," said Timothy. "Now we need clown outfits. Let's look around and see what we can find to wear."

As they were looking around, they found a box of old clothes. Many of the things in the box were faded and patched. Of course, most of the clothes were too small for Dumbo—and most of them were too big for Timothy.

But there were lots of things to choose from—baggy trousers, striped pajamas, bright-colored shirts, big shoes, work gloves, and all kinds of hats.

"Oh, boy!" said Timothy. "Let's try on some of these, Dumbo."

Dumbo put on a shirt and pants that were much too small. He tied a big, funny bow under his collar and put a tiny hat on his head. Timothy looked at him and laughed.

"That's a good clown outfit," said Timothy. "You really do look funny."

Next Timothy tried on some clothes he found for himself. The pants were baggy and the shirt sleeves were so long that they flapped. And Timothy's shoes were much too big! Dumbo looked at Timothy and giggled.

Find some old clothes and make a funny clown costume for yourself like Dumbo and Timothy did. Your costume will be even funnier if some of the clothes are too large or too small for you.

17

Be a Clown

Dumbo and Timothy knew that if they were going to be funny clowns, they would need to plan a clown act. Dumbo had to make up a happy clown act to match the face he had painted. And Timothy had to make up a sad clown act to go with his sad clown face.

Dumbo didn't have much trouble acting happy, because most of the time he *was* happy. He started his act by turning lots of somersaults. (Dumbo's somersaults were slightly above the ground.) He laughed a lot. He jumped up and down and did a little dance.

Timothy thought Dumbo looked so funny that he laughed out loud—but, of course, Timothy didn't look like he was laughing. He was wearing his sad clown face. Then it was time for Timothy to do his act. He got out a big old handkerchief and pretended to cry into it. Then he sneezed, "Kerchoo!" Timothy opened the handkerchief, and there was a big hole right in the middle of it. (Of course, Timothy had made the hole ahead of time.) Dumbo laughed until a tear rolled down his cheek.

The Swing

How do you like to go up in a swing,
 Up in the air so blue?
Oh, I do think it the pleasantest thing
 Ever a child can do!

Up in the air and over the wall,
 Till I can see so wide,
Rivers and trees and cattle and all
 Over the countryside—

Till I look down on the garden green,
 Down on the roof so brown—
Up in the air I go flying again,
 Up in the air and down!

—Robert Louis Stevenson

Confetti Corn

One day Dumbo looked down from high up in the
circus tent and saw a popcorn vendor selling popcorn to
the boys and girls at the circus. Suddenly, Dumbo felt
very hungry—and he just couldn't control himself. After
all, popcorn was his favorite snack. He swooped down
over the vendor, and the vendor reached up and gave
him a bag of popcorn.

"This is my own special popcorn," the vendor called.
"Try it, Dumbo."

Dumbo looked into his bag of popcorn. It certainly
was special! The white, fluffy popcorn was speckled
with all sorts of colors. It looked just like confetti!

You can make the popcorn vendor's special confetti
corn. The directions are on the next page.

What you'll need

Popping corn (light kernels work best)

Red, blue, and green food coloring

Three paper cups

Paper towels

Spoons

Popcorn popper, or pan with tight lid

Oil for popper (if needed)

Large bowl

Salt (if needed)

1. Pour a good handful of popping corn into each cup.

2. Add 40 or 50 drops of food coloring to each cup. Stir each cup of popping corn and coloring with a different spoon, until the kernels are well coated.

3. Let the cups sit for three or four hours. Stir each cup now and then.

4. Spread each cup of popping corn on a paper towel. Let the color dry for at least an hour.

5. When the kernels are dry, use the colored popping corn and oil to make popcorn. Follow the directions for your popcorn popper, or put the oil and popping corn in a tightly covered pan and pop it on the stove at low heat.

6. Pour the popcorn into a large bowl. Salt the popcorn lightly if you like it that way.

Jiminy Cricket says, "Ask for help when popping the corn."

Now You See It!
Now You Don't!

Dumbo and Timothy went from tent to tent, looking for Zircus the Circus Magician. They wanted to watch him practice his magic tricks for the evening show.

When they found him, he was just finishing breakfast. "Hello, Dumbo and Timothy," he said. "Come in."

Zircus handed Dumbo and Timothy a sheet of paper. "Someone left a message for you," he said.

Dumbo and Timothy looked at the paper. It was blank! "There's nothing on it," said Timothy. "How can we read a message that isn't there?"

"There's a message on the paper, all right," said Zircus. "Give the paper back to me and I'll show you the message." The magician took the paper. Then he turned on the toaster and held the paper over it for a few seconds. Dumbo and Timothy saw the message, "I love the circus," appear right before their eyes.

"That's a good trick," said Timothy. "How did you do it?"

Of course, the magician wouldn't tell. But here's the secret: He used a toothpick dipped in lemon juice to write the message. Then he let the lemon juice dry. Dumbo and Timothy couldn't see the message, because the dried lemon juice had no color. But when the paper was heated, the lemon juice turned brown and the message appeared.

Jiminy Cricket says, "Ask a grown-up to help you heat the paper."

"I'll show you some card tricks as soon as I pick up these cards," Zircus told them. He put his hand down flat on the table and slipped two cards under it. Then he slipped in two more . . . and two more . . . until there were ten cards under his hand. He waved his magic wand over his hand and said, "Zircus-workus!" He lifted his hand slowly, and the ten cards came up with it.

You can do Zircus' card trick, too. Just follow the directions on the next page. Be sure to practice the trick before you show it to friends.

What you'll need
Ring
"Magic wand" (a long,
  straight stick)
Toothpick
Table
Ten cards

1. Before you do the trick, put the ring on
   your finger. Slip a toothpick under the
   ring. Be sure that the toothpick sticks out
   on both sides—half pointing along your
   finger and half pointing toward your palm.
   When you do the trick, move your hand
   naturally—but keep the toothpick hidden.

2. Explain that you are going to pick up the
   cards. Put your hand on the table, palm
   down. Slip one card under your fingers
   and one card under your palm, between
   the toothpick and your hand. Then slip the
   other cards in, one at a time, between the
   first two cards and your hand. The first
   two cards will hold the other eight cards in
   place.

3. Say "hocus pocus" (or a magic word of your
   own) and wave your wand over your hand.
   Then slowly raise your hand from the
   table. The cards will rise with your hand.
   Keep your hand flat, so that the toothpick
   stays hidden.

4. Finish the trick by pulling the "stuck" cards
   off with your other hand. Let your friends
   look at them and try to figure out the trick.
   While they are looking, slide the toothpick
   out of the ring and hide it!

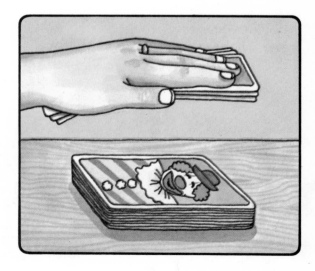

What Has a Trunk?

What is large and gray and has 8 wheels and a trunk?

Dumbo on roller skates.

What is the difference between an elephant and a flea?

An elephant can have fleas but a flea can't have elephants.

What time is it when an elephant sits on the fence?

Time to get the fence fixed.

Why did the elephant walk to New York?

They wouldn't let him take a trunk on the airplane.

What is brown and has big ears and a trunk?

Timothy going on vacation.

How can you tell if an elephant has been sleeping in your bed?

Look for some peanut shells under your pillow.

Why won't an elephant wear purple pajamas?

It would look too much like a grape.

Balloon Fun

"I love balloons," said Timothy. "Let's stop and see the balloon man. Maybe he'll give us a balloon to play with."

The balloon man did something even better than that! He made a duck puppet out of balloons and gave it to Dumbo and Timothy. Of course, he showed them how to make their puppet dance and bow. He even made the duck fly. Dumbo and Timothy liked their duck puppet so much that they made another one just like it.

You can make a balloon puppet, too. Just do what Dumbo and Timothy did.

What you'll need

2 round balloons   Construction paper
String   Plastic drinking straws
Clear tape

1. Blow up the balloons. Make one balloon
   larger than the other. Tie the balloons
   together at the knots.

2. Cut 4 small triangles and 2 large triangles
   from yellow construction paper. The size of
   the triangles will depend on the size of the
   balloons.

3. Use a small triangle for the beak. Trim one
   corner into a rounded shape. Tape it to the
   small balloon. Use another small triangle
   for a tail. Round off two corners and tape
   it to the back of the large balloon. Then
   add two large triangles for wings.

4. Cut and tape on small circles for eyes and a
   paper fringe for eyelashes.

5. Cut a piece of string 16 inches (41
   centimeters) long. Turn the duck over and
   tape the center of the string to the large
   balloon. Then thread each end of the string
   through a 4-inch (10-cm) piece of drinking
   straw.

6. Trim the last two triangles as shown to
   make the duck's feet. Tape each end of the
   string to a foot.

7. Cut a piece of string about 3 feet (91 cm)
   long. Tape the string to the duck's back
   and head. Thread one end of the string
   through a 4-inch (10-cm) piece of straw and
   tie the ends together. Center the straw on
   the string and use it to make the puppet
   move.

31

You can make your duck puppet do tricks. Hold the drinking-straw handle and raise the duck until its feet are flat on the floor or a table. Jerk the handle up and down quickly, and the duck will dance.

Tip the handle toward the front of the duck. Your duck will bow.

Raise the puppet so that the duck's feet are in the air. Hold the duck out at arm's length and turn around and around. The duck will fly around you in a circle.

"Your ducks need something to eat," the balloon man said. "I'll make some apples for them." He took some red and green balloons out of his pocket and made balloon apples. Here's how to do it.

What you'll need

Long balloons (about 6 inches
  or 15 centimeters)

1. Blow up the balloon just a little and tie a knot in the neck. You should be able to move the air from end to end by squeezing the ends of the balloon.

2. Squeeze most of the air up to the knotted end. There should be a long, soft tail on the end opposite the knot.

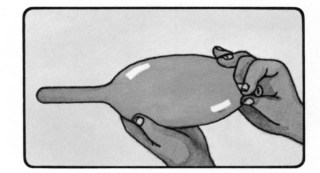

3. Stick your finger in the neck of the balloon where the knot is. Poke the knot up into the tail of the balloon. Use your other hand to pinch the knot through the balloon tail. Take your finger out of the balloon neck.

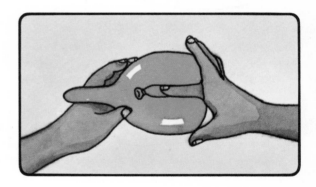

4. Hold the knot inside the tail and twist the balloon toward you. Keep twisting until the balloon is hard and the knot stays in place when you let go of it. The knot in the tail is the apple stem.

The Wild Animal Show

One day, as Dumbo and Timothy were passing the wild animal cage, they saw the lion tamer sitting inside. He was all alone, and he looked very sad. "What's the matter?" Timothy asked the lion tamer.

"All of my lions have bad colds, and they won't be able to perform today," the lion tamer told them. "Without my lions, I have no act."

"Dumbo and I will help you," said Timothy. "You wait here. We'll be right back."

Timothy got some brown paper bags. First he cut two strips from around the top of a bag—one large enough to go around Dumbo's head and one small enough to go around his own. Then he cut rows of long, medium, and short fringe from more brown bags. He pasted them onto the strips, with the longest fringe on the bottom. Then he stapled a piece of yarn to each end of the strip.

"Now we have manes," said Timothy as he and Dumbo tied the yarn under their chins.

The lion tamer held up a large hoop. Dumbo flapped his ears and flew through it. Then Timothy rolled over and over on the floor. Both of them sat up on stools, roared, and did all the other things lions do (although Timothy couldn't really roar very loud).

"I don't think we fooled anyone," Timothy said later. "The people knew we weren't lions."

"That doesn't matter," the lion tamer said. "They liked our act anyway. Thanks for helping me."

Up and Down the Midway

"Pitch a penny in a plate! Win a prize!" a barker shouted as Dumbo and Timothy walked along the midway.

"Knock the bottles down!" shouted another barker.

Still another barker shouted, "Ring toss! Ring toss!"

Timothy and Dumbo played all the games. Timothy liked pitching pennies best of all. He even won a prize when his penny landed in a plate.

You can make your own midway and invite your friends to try their skill. Give balloons, ribbons, or homemade treats away as prizes.

Knock the Bottle Down

Partly fill five plastic bottles with sand or marbles. (This will keep the bottles from tipping over too easily.) Players stand behind a line and throw balls at the bottles to try to knock them down.

Bottle Ringtoss

Use more sand-filled bottles. Line them up, leaving enough space for rings to fall between them. Cut large rings from an empty plastic bleach bottle. Players try to toss the rings around the bottles.

Penny Pitch

Put boxes of different heights on the floor and set a paper plate on each. Players pitch pennies into the plates.

Penny Pitch Challenge

Float a plastic food dish in a dishpan full of water. Players pitch pennies into the floating dish.

Jiminy Cricket says, "Ask a grown-up to help you cut the bleach bottle."

37

Show Time!

Hurry! Hurry! The show is about to begin. Find your way from the ticket booth to the Big Top, where Dumbo and Timothy are performing. Trace the path with your finger.

Juggle Up!

Timothy enjoyed riding in Dumbo's hat, but he wanted to do a circus act of his own. He wanted to learn to juggle! So Timothy and Dumbo went to see one of the circus jugglers.

"Why, of course I can teach you to juggle, Timothy," the juggler told him. "It takes a lot of practice, but it's a lot of fun, too. Why don't we begin right now?"

So Timothy had his first juggling lesson. He practiced hard. He did learn to juggle—and it *was* lots of fun.

Here are some of the things he learned.

Flip and Catch

Stand with your hands in front of your waist. Hold a ball in the palm of your hand. Flip the ball from one hand to the other. Make the ball go in a graceful curve no higher than your eyes.

Don't raise your hand to catch the ball—just let the ball fall into your hand. Then flip the ball back. Keep flipping the ball back and forth, no higher than eye level, until you get used to using either hand.

Flip One, Hold One

Put two balls in the hand you use to write. Hold one
ball in the palm of your hand with your little finger and
third finger. Hold the other ball with your thumb and
first two fingers. Practice flipping the ball you are
holding with the thumb and fingers from hand to hand.

Flip One, Hold Two

Hold a third ball in the hand you *don't* use to write,
using your little finger and third finger. Hold the first
two balls in your writing hand. Practice flipping the
thumb-and-fingers ball from hand to hand while you
hold the other two balls.

Two-Ball Catch

Put two balls in the hand you use to write—and put your other hand behind your back. Toss the thumb-and-fingers ball up about two feet (60 centimeters) above your head. As the ball starts to come down, move your hand slightly to the right and toss the other ball. Move your hand a little to the left to catch the first ball with your fingertips. Then move your hand to the right and catch the second ball.

Practice catching with your writing hand until you can catch both balls almost every time. Then practice catching with the other hand. It won't be as easy with that hand, but keep trying!

Two-Handed Juggling

When you can throw and catch well with either hand, you're ready to try juggling with both hands. To begin, toss and catch one ball with your writing hand several times. Get a rhythm going. Then toss the ball across to the other hand. While the ball is in the air, use your other hand to flip the second ball into your writing hand and then catch the first ball.

Now throw the second ball with your writing hand. Use your other hand to flip the first ball and catch the second ball. Try to keep the toss-flip-catch rhythm going. With practice, you can make the balls go round and round.